CONTENTS

CHAPTER 1:
INTRODUCTION

The Power of Excel Formulas

In the vast world of data analysis, financial modeling, and everyday administrative tasks, Microsoft Excel stands as an unrivaled pillar. It's not just the gridlines, the cells, or the rows and columns that make Excel powerful; it's the formulas. Excel formulas breathe life into spreadsheets, turning a static table of numbers into a dynamic and powerful tool for decision-making.

OBJECTIVE OF
THIS BOOK

This book, "Master Excel: Top 100 Formulas and How-Tos," aims to empower both the novice and the adept user. By diving deep into 100 of the most pivotal formulas, we'll unravel their mysteries, showcase real-world applications, and provide step-by-step guides for practical implementations.

WHY MASTER EXCEL FORMULAS?

- **Efficiency:** Speed up tasks that would typically take hours to complete manually.

- **Accuracy:** Reduce human errors by automating calculations.

- **Insight:** Derive meaningful insights from raw data, helping in informed decision-making.

- **Skill Enhancement:** Excel proficiency is a sought-after skill in many professions, from finance to marketing to administration.

WHO IS THIS BOOK FOR?

Whether you're just starting out with Excel or consider yourself a seasoned pro, there's always something new to learn. This book caters to:

- **Beginners:** Understand the basics and build a strong foundation.

- **Intermediate Users:** Enhance your skills and learn advanced techniques.

- **Experts:** Discover nuances and efficiencies that can make complex tasks simpler.

A JOURNEY THROUGH EXCEL'S CAPABILITIES

From basic arithmetic to complex financial modeling, from simple text manipulations to sophisticated lookup functions, we will journey through the myriad capabilities of Excel formulas. By the end of this book, you will have a toolkit of formulas and the knowledge to apply them effectively.

CHAPTER 2: BASIC ARITHMETIC FORMULAS

Arithmetic operations form the backbone of any data analysis, allowing us to derive meaningful numbers and statistics from raw data. In this chapter, we'll explore some of Excel's fundamental arithmetic formulas that can aid in various calculations.

SUM

Description:
The SUM function adds up all the numbers in a specified range.

Real-World Example:
Imagine you're a teacher who wants to calculate the total marks obtained by a student in a series of tests. Instead of adding each test score manually, you can use the SUM function to get the total effortlessly.

Step-by-step Implementation:

1. Click on the cell where you want the total marks to appear.

2. Type **=SUM(** followed by the range of cells containing the test scores. For instance, if the scores are in cells A1 through A10, the formula would be **=SUM(A1:A10)**.

3. Press Enter.

4. The cell will now display the total marks obtained by the student across all tests.

Variations:

- **Cell-by-cell Addition:** Instead of using a range, you can individually add specific cells. For instance, **=A1+B1+C1** would add the values of cells A1, B1, and C1.

- **Using Constants:** You can add a constant value to a range. For example, **=SUM(A1:A10)+5** would add all values in the range A1:A10 and then add 5 to the total.

- **Multiple Ranges:** The SUM function can handle multiple ranges. For example, **=SUM(A1:A5, C1:C5)** would sum values from both the specified ranges.

AVERAGE

Description:

The AVERAGE function calculates the average (arithmetic mean) of the numbers in a specified range.

Real-World Example:

Suppose you're a sports coach and want to determine the average score of a player over several matches. Instead of manually adding each score and then dividing by the number of matches, you can use the AVERAGE function to quickly find out the player's average score.

Step-by-step Implementation:

1. Click on the cell where you want the average score to appear.

2. Type **=AVERAGE(** followed by the range of cells containing the scores. For instance, if the scores are in cells B1 through B10, the formula would be **=AVERAGE(B1:B10)**.

3. Press Enter.

4. The cell will now display the average score of the player across the matches.

Variations:

- **Ignoring Zero:** If you want to calculate the average without considering zero values, you can use a combination of SUM and COUNTIF: **=SUM(B1:B10)/ COUNTIF(B1:B10, "<>0")**.

- **Weighted Average:** If each score has a weight (importance), you might not want a simple average. In such cases, you'd multiply each score by its weight, sum those products, and then divide by the sum of weights.

- **AVERAGEA:** This function calculates the average of values in a range, including numbers, text, and logical values. For instance, TRUE is considered as 1 and FALSE as 0.

MIN

Description:
The MIN function returns the smallest value from a set of values.

Real-World Example:
Imagine you're a store manager tracking daily sales. You want to identify the day with the lowest sales in a given month to understand anomalies or factors that might have affected business on that particular day.

Step-by-step Implementation:
1. Click on the cell where you want the lowest sales value to appear.

2. Type =**MIN(** followed by the range of cells containing the daily sales. If the sales are listed in cells C1 through C30 for a month, the formula would be =**MIN(C1:C30)**.

3. Press Enter.

4. The cell will now display the lowest sales value for the given month.

Variations:
- **Specific Criteria:** If you want to find the minimum value based on a specific criteria, you can combine the MIN function with an array formula. For example, to find the lowest sale on a weekend, you might use a formula like =**MIN(IF((WEEKDAY(D1:D30,2)>5), C1:C30))**, where column D contains the corresponding dates.

- **Ignoring Zero:** To find the minimum value that isn't zero, you can use an array formula like =**MIN(IF(C1:C30<>0, C1:C30))**.

- **MINA:** This function returns the smallest value in a set of values, considering numbers, text, and logical values. For instance, TRUE is considered as 1 and FALSE as 0.

MAX

Description:
The MAX function returns the largest value from a set of values.

Real-World Example:
Imagine you're a fitness trainer tracking the progress of an athlete's sprint times. You want to identify their slowest sprint time during a training session to analyze areas of improvement.

Step-by-step Implementation:
1. Click on the cell where you want the slowest sprint time to appear.
2. Type **=MAX(** followed by the range of cells containing the sprint times. If the times are listed in cells D1 through D10 for a session, the formula would be **=MAX(D1:D10)**.
3. Press Enter.
4. The cell will now display the slowest sprint time for the given session.

Variations:
- **Specific Criteria:** If you want to find the maximum value based on a specific criteria, you can combine the MAX function with an array formula. For example, to find the slowest time on a rainy day, you might use a formula like **=MAX(IF(E1:E10="Rainy", D1:D10))**, where column E denotes the weather condition on the respective days.

- **Ignoring Zero:** To find the maximum value that isn't zero, you can use an array formula like **=MAX(IF(D1:D10<>0, D1:D10))**.

- **MAXA:** This function returns the largest value in a set of values, considering numbers, text, and logical values.

11

For instance, TRUE is considered as 1 and FALSE as 0.

PRODUCT

Description:
The PRODUCT function multiplies all the numbers in a specified range and returns the result.

Real-World Example:
Imagine you run an online store and want to calculate the total earnings from selling a particular product. You'd multiply the number of units sold by the price per unit.

Step-by-step Implementation:
1. In one cell (say A1), enter the number of units sold.

2. In another cell (say B1), enter the price per unit.

3. Click on a cell where you want the total earnings to appear.

4. Type =**PRODUCT(A1, B1)**.

5. Press Enter.

6. The cell will now display the total earnings from the product.

Variations:
- **Range Multiplication:** Instead of specifying individual cells, you can multiply a range of cells. For instance, if you have a series of multipliers in cells C1 through C5, you can use =**PRODUCT(C1:C5)** to get the result of multiplying all those numbers.

- **Including Constants:** You can multiply a range by a constant. For example, =**PRODUCT(A1:A10, 10)** would multiply all the values in A1:A10 by 10.

- **Nested Multiplication:** If you want to multiply the results of other calculations, you can nest functions within PRODUCT. For example, **=PRODUCT(SUM(D1:D5), AVERAGE(E1:E5))** multiplies the sum of D1:D5 by the average of E1:E5.

COUNT

Description:
The COUNT function returns the number of cells in a range that contain numbers.

Real-World Example:
Imagine you're an event planner and you've listed down the number of attendees for each event in a series of cells. Some cells might be empty or have text entries like "TBD". You want to know how many events have a specified number of attendees.

Step-by-step Implementation:
1. Assume the number of attendees for various events are listed in cells F1 through F20.

2. Click on a cell where you want the count of events with specified attendees to appear.

3. Type **=COUNT(F1:F20)**.

4. Press Enter.

5. The cell will display the count of events that have a number in the F1:F20 range, ignoring empty cells or cells with non-numeric entries.

Variations:
- **Counting Non-Empty Cells:** To count all non-empty cells, regardless of whether they contain numbers or text, use the COUNTA function: **=COUNTA(F1:F20)**.

- **Counting Based on Criteria:** If you want to count cells based on specific criteria, like counting all events with more than 50 attendees, you'd use the COUNTIF function: **=COUNTIF(F1:F20, ">50")**.

- **Counting With Multiple Criteria:** To count based on

multiple conditions, like events with attendees between 50 and 100, you'd use the COUNTIFS function: **=COUNTIFS(F1:F20, ">50", F1:F20, "<100")**

AVERAGEIF

Description:

The AVERAGEIF function calculates the average of numbers in a range based on a single specified criterion.

Real-World Example:

Imagine you're a teacher and you want to calculate the average score of students who scored above 70 in a test. The AVERAGEIF function can help you quickly determine this average without manually filtering or sorting data.

Step-by-step Implementation:

1. Assume students' scores are listed in cells G1 through G30.

2. Click on a cell where you want the average of scores above 70 to appear.

3. Type **=AVERAGEIF(G1:G30, ">70")**.

4. Press Enter.

5. The cell will display the average score of students who scored more than 70.

Variations:

- **Criteria with Text:** If you have a list of grades (like A, B, C) in cells H1 through H30 and want to find the average score of students with grade "A", use: **=AVERAGEIF(H1:H30, "A", G1:G30)**.

- **Including a Range for Averages:** You can specify a different range for the averages. For example, if G1:G30 has scores and I1:I30 has corresponding bonus points, to get the average bonus points for scores above 70, use: **=AVERAGEIF(G1:G30, ">70", I1:I30)**.

- **Multiple Conditions:** For more complex criteria, like finding the average score of students who scored between 50 and 70, you'd use the AVERAGEIFS function: **=AVERAGEIFS(G1:G30, G1:G30, ">50", G1:G30, "<70").**

MOD

Description:
The MOD function returns the remainder of a division operation between two numbers.

Real-World Example:
Imagine you're managing a warehouse and you have boxes that can contain 12 items each. You have a shipment of 257 items. You want to know how many items will be in the last partially filled box after you've packed as many full boxes as possible.

Step-by-step Implementation:
1. In cell J1, enter the total number of items: 257.

2. In cell J2, enter the capacity of each box: 12.

3. Click on a cell where you want the number of items in the last partially filled box to appear.

4. Type **=MOD(J1, J2)**.

5. Press Enter.

6. The cell will display the number of items (5 in this case) that will be in the last box.

Variations:
- **Determining Even or Odd:** You can use the MOD function to determine if a number is even or odd. For a number in cell K1, the formula **=MOD(K1, 2)** will return 0 for even numbers and 1 for odd numbers.

- **Rotating Values:** If you have a set of rotating tasks assigned to a team and you want to know who will handle the task on day X, you can use the MOD function. If there are 7 team members and it's day 45, **=MOD(45, 7)** will tell you it's the 3rd member's turn.

- **Cycling Through Lists:** MOD can be used to cycle through lists. For example, if you have a list of colors and want to assign them in a repeating sequence to items, MOD can help you determine which color to assign next.

ROUND

Description:
The ROUND function rounds a number to a specified number of digits.

Real-World Example:
You're an accountant and have calculated the monthly interest on an investment as $456.789. For reporting purposes, you want to round this to two decimal places, representing cents.

Step-by-step Implementation:
1. Assume the calculated interest is in cell L1.

2. Click on a cell where you want the rounded interest value to appear.

3. Type **=ROUND(L1, 2)**.

4. Press Enter.

5. The cell will now display the rounded interest value as $456.79.

Variations:
- **Rounding to Whole Numbers:** If you want to round to the nearest whole number, you can use **=ROUND(L1, 0)**.

- **Rounding to Tens, Hundreds, etc.:** For rounding to the nearest ten, use **=ROUND(L1, -1)**. For hundreds, use **=ROUND(L1, -2)**, and so on.

- **Other Rounding Functions:**
    - **ROUNDUP:** Always rounds up, away from zero.
    - **ROUNDDOWN:** Always rounds down, towards zero.
    - **MROUND:** Rounds to the nearest specified multiple.

ABS

Description:
The ABS function returns the absolute value of a number. It converts negative numbers to positive, while positive numbers remain unchanged.

Real-World Example:
Imagine you're analyzing stock market data and you want to determine the magnitude of a stock's price change without considering whether it went up or down. The ABS function can help you focus solely on the size of the change.

Step-by-step Implementation:
1. Assume the daily change in stock price is in cell M1, which might be a positive or negative value.

2. Click on a cell where you want the absolute change in price to appear.

3. Type =**ABS(M1)**.

4. Press Enter.

5. The cell will display the magnitude of the stock's price change as a positive number.

Variations:
- **Comparing Magnitudes:** If you want to compare the magnitudes of changes between two stocks, you can use the ABS function for both and then compare the results. For instance, **=ABS(M1) > ABS(N1)** would check if the magnitude of the change in stock M is greater than that of stock N.

- **Conditional Formatting Based on Magnitude:** You can use the ABS function in conditional formatting rules to, for example, highlight cells where the magnitude of a value exceeds a certain threshold.

- **Determining Average Magnitude of Change:** If you have a series of changes in cells M1 through M10 and want to find the average magnitude, you can use **=AVERAGE(ABS(M1:M10))**.

SQRT

Description:
The SQRT function returns the positive square root of a number.

Real-World Example:
You're a civil engineer planning to build a square park. You know the park's total area, but you need to find out the length of one side to design the boundary. The SQRT function can help you determine this length.

Step-by-step Implementation:
1. Assume the total area of the park is in cell N1.

2. Click on a cell where you want the length of one side of the park to appear.

3. Type **=SQRT(N1)**.

4. Press Enter.

5. The cell will display the length of one side of the square park.

Variations:
- **Square Root of Differences:** If you want to find the square root of the difference between two values, you can use **=SQRT(ABS(O1-P1))**, where O1 and P1 are the two values.

- **Hypotenuse Calculation:** The SQRT function can be used in the Pythagorean theorem to determine the hypotenuse of a right triangle. If A and B are the lengths of the two shorter sides, the hypotenuse C can be found using **=SQRT(A^2 + B^2)**.

- **Roots Other Than Square:** For cube roots or other nth roots, you can use the POWER function. For a cube root,

=POWER(Q1, 1/3) would return the cube root of the value in Q1.

EXP

Description:
The EXP function returns the result of the constant e raised to the power of a given number. The value of e is approximately 2.71828.

Real-World Example:
You're studying biology and are examining bacterial growth, which often follows an exponential growth pattern. Given the growth rate, you can use the EXP function to predict how much a bacteria population might increase over a certain period.

Step-by-step Implementation:
1. Assume the growth rate over one hour for a bacteria colony is in cell O1.

2. To predict the growth over 5 hours, click on a cell where you want the growth multiplier to appear.

3. Type =**EXP(5*O1)**.

4. Press Enter.

5. The cell will now display the growth multiplier for the bacteria over 5 hours.

Variations:
- **Exponential Decay:** In fields like physics and chemistry, exponential decay (like radioactive decay) can be modeled using the EXP function in combination with negative values.

- **Natural Logarithm:** The inverse of the EXP function is the natural logarithm, given by the LN function in Excel. It computes the power to which e must be raised to produce a given number.

POWER

Description:
The POWER function returns the result of a number raised to a specified power.

Real-World Example:
You're a financial analyst projecting the growth of an investment. To calculate compound interest, you need to raise the base amount by a certain power based on the rate of return and the number of periods.

Step-by-step Implementation:
1. Assume the base amount (initial investment) is in cell P1 and the rate of return is in cell Q1.

2. To project the growth over 5 years, click on a cell where you want the projected amount to appear.

3. Type **=P1 * POWER(1 + Q1, 5)**.

4. Press Enter.

5. The cell will now display the projected amount after 5 years based on compound interest.

Variations:
- **Square and Cube:** For squaring a number, you can use **=POWER(R1, 2)**. For cubing a number, use **=POWER(R1, 3)**.

- **Roots:** The POWER function can also compute nth roots. For instance, to find the fourth root of a number in cell S1, you'd use **=POWER(S1, 0.25)**.

- **Inverse Power:** To compute the inverse of a number raised to a power (useful in some scientific calculations), you can use a negative exponent, like **=POWER(T1, -2)** for the inverse square of T1.

CHAPTER 3: DATE & TIME FORMULAS

Working with dates and times in Excel can seem daunting, especially given the software's unique date system. However, with a good understanding of Excel's date and time functions, you can easily manage, analyze, and manipulate temporal data. This chapter will introduce you to some of the most commonly used date and time functions, helping you harness the full potential of Excel for any time-sensitive task.

We'll start with the **TODAY** function:

TODAY

Description:
The TODAY function returns the current date.

Real-World Example:
You're managing a project and want to automatically keep track of the current date to determine deadlines, pending tasks, or elapsed time since the project's start.

Step-by-step Implementation:
1. Click on a cell where you want the current date to appear.
2. Type =**TODAY()**.
3. Press Enter.
4. The cell will now display the current date, and it will update automatically each day you open the spreadsheet.

Variations:
- **Adding/Subtracting Days:** To get a date that's 10 days after today, you can use =**TODAY() + 10**. For 10 days before, use =**TODAY() - 10**.

- **Combining with Other Functions:** You can use the TODAY function within other formulas. For instance, to determine the number of days between today and a given end date in cell U1, you'd use =**U1 - TODAY()**.

NOW

Description:
The NOW function returns the current date and time.

Real-World Example:
You're running a customer support center, and you want to timestamp when each inquiry arrives to track response times and ensure timely support.

Step-by-step Implementation:
1. Click on a cell where you want the current date and time to appear.

2. Type **=NOW()**.

3. Press Enter.

4. The cell will now display the current date and time, and it will update automatically each time the spreadsheet recalculates.

Variations:

- **Extracting Only the Time:** If you're interested only in the current time and not the date, you can use **=MOD(NOW(), 1)**.

- **Adding/Subtracting Hours:** To get a timestamp that's 5 hours after the current time, you can use **=NOW() + 5/24**. Since there are 24 hours in a day, dividing by 24 allows you to adjust by hours.

- **Rounding Time:** If you want to round the time to the nearest hour, you can use **=ROUND(NOW()*24,0)/24**.

DATEDIF

Description:
The DATEDIF function calculates the difference between two dates in terms of days, months, or years.

Real-World Example:
You're in human resources and want to determine the tenure of an employee in the company. By comparing the employee's start date to the current date, you can find out how long they've been with the organization.

Step-by-step Implementation:
1. Assume the employee's start date is in cell V1.
2. Click on a cell where you want the tenure (in years) to appear.
3. Type **=DATEDIF(V1, TODAY(), "y")**.
4. Press Enter.
5. The cell will display the number of complete years between the start date and today.

Variations:
- **Months Difference:** To get the difference in complete months, use **=DATEDIF(V1, TODAY(), "m")**.
- **Days Difference:** For the difference in days, use **=DATEDIF(V1, TODAY(), "d")**.
- **Year and Month Combination:** To find out years and months separately (like "2 years and 5 months"), you can combine two DATEDIF functions: **=DATEDIF(V1, TODAY(), "y") & " years and " & DATEDIF(V1, TODAY(), "ym") & " months"**.
- **Leap Year Consideration:** DATEDIF takes leap years into

account when calculating differences.

DAY, MONTH, YEAR

Description:
The DAY, MONTH, and YEAR functions extract the day, month, or year from a given date, respectively.

Real-World Example:
You're organizing monthly team meetings, and you have a list of dates for each meeting. You want to quickly determine the month or year of each meeting to help in your planning.

Step-by-step Implementation for MONTH:
1. Assume one of the meeting dates is in cell W1.

2. Click on a cell where you want the month of the meeting to appear.

3. Type **=MONTH(W1)**.

4. Press Enter.

5. The cell will display the month number (e.g., 1 for January, 2 for February, etc.) corresponding to the meeting date.

Variations:
- **Extracting Day:** To get the day from a date, use the DAY function: **=DAY(W1)**. This will return the day of the month (from 1 to 31).

- **Extracting Year:** To retrieve the year from a date, use the YEAR function: **=YEAR(W1)**.

- **Combining for Custom Formats:** You can combine these functions to create custom date formats. For example, **=DAY(W1) & "/" & MONTH(W1) & "/" & YEAR(W1)** would return a date in the format "day/month/year".

EOMONTH

Description:
The EOMONTH function returns the last day (end-of-month date) of the month a specified number of months before or after a given start date.

Real-World Example:
You're a financial analyst preparing monthly reports. For each report, you want to highlight the end date of the month, especially when planning for quarterly or yearly closing periods.

Step-by-step Implementation:
1. Assume the start date is in cell X1.

2. Click on a cell where you want the end date of the month (that includes the start date) to appear.

3. Type =**EOMONTH(X1, 0)**.

4. Press Enter.

5. The cell will display the end date of the month for the date in X1.

Variations:
- **Future or Past Months:** The second argument in EOMONTH determines how many months before or after the start date you want to consider. For example, to get the end date of the next month, use =**EOMONTH(X1, 1)**. To get the end date of the previous month, use =**EOMONTH(X1, -1)**.

- **Quarterly Closing:** If you want to find the end date of the quarter, you can use a combination of MONTH and EOMONTH functions. For instance, to get the end date of the current quarter, you could use: =EOMONTH(X1,

CHOOSE(MATCH(MONTH(X1), {1,4,7,10}), 2, 5, 8, 11) - MONTH(X1))

WEEKDAY

Description:
The WEEKDAY function returns the day of the week for a given date as a number (1 for Sunday, 2 for Monday, and so on, up to 7 for Saturday).

Real-World Example:
You're managing a team and have a policy that no meetings should be scheduled on Fridays. Before setting a date for the next team meeting, you want to check the day of the week to ensure you're adhering to this policy.

Step-by-step Implementation:
1. Assume the proposed date for the meeting is in cell Y1.
2. Click on a cell where you want the day of the week to appear.
3. Type **=WEEKDAY(Y1)**.
4. Press Enter.
5. The cell will display a number representing the day of the week. If it displays "6," that means the proposed date is a Friday.

Variations:
- **Custom Starting Day:** By default, WEEKDAY considers Sunday as the first day of the week. However, if you want Monday as the starting day (1 for Monday, 2 for Tuesday, etc.), use **=WEEKDAY(Y1, 2)**.

- **Returning Day Name:** If you'd prefer the name of the day instead of a number, you can combine WEEKDAY with the CHOOSE function: **=CHOOSE(WEEKDAY(Y1, 2), "Monday", "Tuesday", "Wednesday", "Thursday", "Friday", "Saturday", "Sunday")**.

- **Checking for Weekends:** To determine if a date falls on a weekend, you can use a formula like =IF(OR(WEEKDAY(Y1)=7, WEEKDAY(Y1)=1), "Weekend", "Weekday").

WORKDAY

Description:
The WORKDAY function returns a date that is a specified number of workdays ahead or behind a given start date. By default, it treats weekends (Saturdays and Sundays) as non-working days, but you can also specify additional holidays.

Real-World Example:
You're a project manager, and you know that a task will take 10 working days to complete. Starting on a particular date, you want to determine the expected completion date, excluding weekends and any public holidays.

Step-by-step Implementation:
1. Assume the start date of the task is in cell Z1.

2. Let's say there are two public holidays during the task period, and they are in cells Z3 and Z4.

3. Click on a cell where you want the completion date to appear.

4. Type **=WORKDAY(Z1, 10, Z3:Z4)**.

5. Press Enter.

6. The cell will display the date when the task is expected to be completed, considering weekends and the specified holidays.

Variations:
- **Without Holidays:** If you don't have any holidays to consider, you can simply use **=WORKDAY(Z1, 10)**.

- **Working Backwards:** To find a start date based on a known end date and a task duration, you can use a negative duration: **=WORKDAY(Z5, -10, Z3:Z4)** where Z5 is the known end date.

- **Custom Weekends:** If your workweek isn't the standard Monday to Friday, you might want to use the **WORKDAY.INTL** function, which allows you to specify which days of the week are considered weekends.

DATEVALUE

Description:

The DATEVALUE function converts a date represented as text into a serial number that Excel recognizes as a date.

Real-World Example:

You've imported data from another system, and some of the dates have been brought in as text rather than date values. This can cause problems with sorting, filtering, and other date-related functions. Using DATEVALUE, you can convert these text dates into proper Excel date format.

Step-by-step Implementation:

1. Assume the text representation of a date is in cell AA1, for instance, "1-Jan-2023".

2. Click on a cell where you want the converted date value to appear.

3. Type **=DATEVALUE(AA1)**.

4. Press Enter.

5. The cell will now display the date value for "1-Jan-2023". Note: Depending on your cell formatting, it might still look like text. You can adjust the cell format to display it as a date.

Variations:

- **Time Values:** If your text also includes a time value, like "1-Jan-2023 12:30 PM", you can combine DATEVALUE with the TIMEVALUE function: **=DATEVALUE(LEFT(AA2, 10)) + TIMEVALUE(MID(AA2, 12, 8))**.

- **Different Date Formats:** DATEVALUE can handle various date formats, but the exact format it recognizes depends on your system's locale settings. For some formats, you might need additional text manipulation functions to rearrange the components before using DATEVALUE.

- **Error Handling:** If DATEVALUE encounters text that it can't convert to a date, it will return an error. You can use the ISERROR function to detect this and handle it appropriately.

TIMEVALUE

Description:
The TIMEVALUE function converts a time represented as text into a decimal fraction that Excel recognizes as a time.

Real-World Example:
You've received a schedule with times listed as text, such as "3:30 PM" or "15:30". To perform calculations or comparisons with these times, you need them in a format that Excel can recognize as a time value.

Step-by-step Implementation:
1. Assume the text representation of a time is in cell AB1, for instance, "15:30".

2. Click on a cell where you want the converted time value to appear.

3. Type **=TIMEVALUE(AB1)**.

4. Press Enter.

5. The cell will now display the time value for "15:30". Note: Depending on your cell formatting, it might still look like a decimal. You can adjust the cell format to display it as a time.

Variations:
- **Combining with DATEVALUE:** If you have a text entry that contains both date and time, like "1-Jan-2023 15:30", you can extract and convert both components using **=DATEVALUE(LEFT(AB2, 10)) + TIMEVALUE(MID(AB2, 12, 5))**.

- **Different Time Formats:** TIMEVALUE can handle various time formats, but it's typically best to stick with a standard "hh:mm" or "hh:mm AM/PM" format.

- **Error Handling:** If TIMEVALUE can't convert the text to a time, it will return an error. You can use functions like IFERROR to handle these situations gracefully.

EDATE

Description:
The EDATE function returns a date that is a specified number of months before or after a given start date.

Real-World Example:
You work in a leasing office, and when signing new lease agreements, you often need to calculate the exact end date of a lease term based on a specified number of months. The EDATE function allows you to quickly determine this end date.

Step-by-step Implementation:
1. Assume the start date of the lease is in cell AC1 and the lease term is 12 months.

2. Click on a cell where you want the lease end date to appear.

3. Type **=EDATE(AC1, 12)**.

4. Press Enter.

5. The cell will now display the date that is exactly 12 months after the start date in AC1.

Variations:
- **Leases with Different Durations:** You can change the second argument in EDATE to adjust the number of months. For instance, for a 6-month lease, use **=EDATE(AC1, 6)**.

- **Calculating Past Dates:** If you want to find a date that's a certain number of months in the past, use a negative number as the second argument, like **=EDATE(AC1, -6)** for 6 months prior.

- **Considering Days:** EDATE only changes the month and

year of dates. If the start date is January 31st and you add one month, the result will be the last day of February (either the 28th or 29th, depending on the year).

NETWORKDAYS

Description:

The NETWORKDAYS function calculates the number of whole workdays between two dates, excluding weekends and optionally specified holidays.

Real-World Example:

You're a project manager overseeing a task that spans multiple days. To calculate the number of actual working days the task will take (excluding weekends and any public holidays), you can use the NETWORKDAYS function.

Step-by-step Implementation:

1. Assume the start date of the task is in cell AD1 and the end date is in AD2.

2. Let's say there are two public holidays during the task period, and they are in cells AD4 and AD5.

3. Click on a cell where you want the number of working days to appear.

4. Type **=NETWORKDAYS(AD1, AD2, AD4:AD5)**.

5. Press Enter.

6. The cell will display the number of workdays between the two dates, excluding the weekends and specified holidays.

Variations:

- **Without Holidays:** If you don't have any holidays to consider, you can simply use **=NETWORKDAYS(AD1, AD2)**.

- **Custom Weekends:** If your workweek isn't the standard Monday to Friday, you might want to use the **NETWORKDAYS.INTL** function, which allows you to specify which days of the week are considered weekends.

- **Including Start and End Dates:** NETWORKDAYS counts both the start and end dates if they fall on workdays. If either date falls on a weekend or specified holiday, it will not be counted.

YEARFRAC

Description:
The YEARFRAC function calculates the fraction of the year represented by the number of whole days between two dates.

Real-World Example:
You're in finance and need to calculate the accrued interest for a bond that uses a day-count basis of 30/360 (each month is treated as having 30 days). Using the YEARFRAC function, you can determine the fraction of the year between the bond's issue date and the current date.

Step-by-step Implementation:
1. Assume the bond's issue date is in cell AE1 and today's date is in cell AE2.

2. Click on a cell where you want the fraction of the year to appear.

3. Type **=YEARFRAC(AE1, AE2, 0)**. The third argument, "0", indicates the 30/360 day-count basis.

4. Press Enter.

5. The cell will display the fraction of the year between the two dates using the 30/360 convention.

Variations:
- **Actual/Actual Basis:** If you want to use the actual number of days between two dates divided by the actual number of days in the year(s) between the dates, use **=YEARFRAC(AE1, AE2, 1)**.

- **Actual/365 Basis:** For a fixed denominator of 365, use **=YEARFRAC(AE1, AE2, 2)**.

- **Actual/360 Basis:** For a fixed denominator of 360, use

=**YEARFRAC(AE1, AE2, 3)**.

- **30/360 (European Method):** Similar to the initial example but using a different method for month-end dates, use =**YEARFRAC(AE1, AE2, 4)**.

DAYS360

Description:
The DAYS360 function returns the number of days between two dates based on a 360-day year, which is often used in financial calculations.

Real-World Example:
You're calculating interest on a loan, and the agreement uses a 360-day year for simplicity in monthly calculations (each month is treated as having 30 days). You can use the DAYS360 function to quickly determine the number of days between the loan's start and end dates for interest calculation.

Step-by-step Implementation:
1. Assume the loan's start date is in cell AF1 and the end date is in AF2.

2. Click on a cell where you want the number of days based on the 360-day year to appear.

3. Type **=DAYS360(AF1, AF2)**.

4. Press Enter.

5. The cell will display the number of days between the two dates using the 30/360 convention.

Variations:
- **European Method:** The standard DAYS360 function uses the U.S. method, which has certain rules for handling end-of-month dates. If you want to use the European method, which has different end-of-month rules, you can add an optional argument: **=DAYS360(AF1, AF2, TRUE)**.

- **Comparison with Actual Days:** For reference, you might also calculate the actual number of days between two dates using a simple subtraction: **=AF2 - AF1**.

HOUR, MINUTE, SECOND

Description:

The HOUR, MINUTE, and SECOND functions extract the hour, minute, or second from a given time value, respectively.

Real-World Example:

You're analyzing call center data and have timestamps of when each call started. By extracting the hour, you can determine which times of the day receive the highest call volume.

Step-by-step Implementation for HOUR:

1. Assume the timestamp of a call is in cell AG1.

2. Click on a cell where you want the hour of the call to appear.

3. Type =**HOUR(AG1)**.

4. Press Enter.

5. The cell will display the hour of the call, where 0 represents 12:00 AM and 23 represents 11:00 PM.

Variations:

- **Extracting Minute:** To get the minute from a time value, use the MINUTE function: =**MINUTE(AG1)**.

- **Extracting Second:** To retrieve the second from a time value, use the SECOND function: =**SECOND(AG1)**.

- **Combining for Custom Outputs:** You can combine these functions to create custom time outputs. For example, =**HOUR(AG1) & ":" & MINUTE(AG1)** would return a format like "13:45" for 1:45 PM.

DATE

Description:
The DATE function returns a serial number of a date based on the year, month, and day values you provide.

Real-World Example:
You're planning an event and have separate columns for the day, month, and year of the event. You want to consolidate these columns into a single date column for easier sorting and filtering.

Step-by-step Implementation:
1. Assume the year of the event is in cell AH1, the month in AH2, and the day in AH3.

2. Click on a cell where you want the consolidated date to appear.

3. Type **=DATE(AH1, AH2, AH3)**.

4. Press Enter.

5. The cell will now display the date corresponding to the provided year, month, and day values.

Variations:
- **Creating Future/Past Dates:** You can use the DATE function with simple arithmetic to get dates in the future or past. For instance, to get a date one year from the date in AI1, use **=DATE(YEAR(AI1) + 1, MONTH(AI1), DAY(AI1))**.

- **Validating Dates:** The DATE function will adjust for invalid dates. For example, if you use **=DATE(2023, 2, 30)**, the function will return March 2, 2023, because February doesn't have 30 days.

- **Combining with TODAY:** To determine your age

based on your birth date in AJ1, you can use =YEAR(TODAY()) - YEAR(AJ1) - IF(MONTH(TODAY()) < MONTH(AJ1) OR (MONTH(TODAY()) = MONTH(AJ1) AND DAY(TODAY()) < DAY(AJ1)), 1, 0).

NOW

Description:
The NOW function returns the current date and time. It's a volatile function, which means it updates every time the worksheet recalculates.

Real-World Example:
You're maintaining a log sheet where you record activities or tasks as they occur. By using the NOW function, you can automatically timestamp each entry with the exact date and time.

Step-by-step Implementation:
1. Click on a cell where you want the current date and time to appear.
2. Type **=NOW()**.
3. Press Enter.
4. The cell will display the current date and time. As the worksheet recalculates (e.g., when you make other changes or manually recalculate), this value will update to the current moment.

Variations:
- **Date Only:** If you only want the current date without the time, you can use the **TODAY** function: **=TODAY()**.
- **Time Only:** To extract only the current time from the NOW function, you can use **=NOW() - TODAY()**.
- **Static Timestamp:** If you want a timestamp that doesn't update every time the worksheet recalculates, you can enter the current date and time without using a formula. In Excel, pressing **Ctrl + ;** inserts the current date, and **Ctrl + Shift + ;** inserts the current time.

CHAPTER 4: LOGICAL FORMULAS

Logical formulas play a vital role in decision-making within Excel sheets. They evaluate specific conditions to return a value or action based on whether the condition is true or false. This chapter covers some of the most widely-used logical functions in Excel.

Let's begin with the **IF** function.

IF

Description:

The IF function allows you to make decisions based on a condition. It evaluates a condition to return one value if the condition is true and another value if it's false.

Real-World Example:

In a sales report, you want to classify sales as either "High" if they exceed $10,000 or "Low" if they don't.

Step-by-step Implementation:

1. Assume the sales value is in cell AM1.

2. Click on a cell where you want the classification to appear.

3. Type =IF(AM1 > 10000, "High", "Low").

4. Press Enter.

5. The cell will display "High" if the sales in AM1 exceed $10,000 and "Low" otherwise.

Variations:

- **Nested IFs:** You can nest multiple IF functions to handle more than two outcomes. For instance, to classify sales as "High", "Medium", or "Low": =IF(AM1 > 10000, "High", IF(AM1 > 5000, "Medium", "Low")).

- **Combining with Other Functions:** IF can be used with other Excel functions to create more complex logic. For instance, with AND: =IF(AND(AM1 > 5000, AM1 <= 10000), "Medium", "Other").

AND & OR

Description:

- **AND:** The AND function evaluates multiple conditions and returns TRUE if all the conditions are true. Otherwise, it returns FALSE.

- **OR:** The OR function evaluates multiple conditions and returns TRUE if at least one of the conditions is true. If none are true, it returns FALSE.

Real-World Example:

You're assessing the performance of sales representatives. A representative is eligible for a bonus if they have made more than 50 sales **AND** if their customer feedback score is above 4.5. Alternatively, they are also eligible if they've been with the company for more than 5 years, regardless of their sales or feedback score.

Step-by-step Implementation for AND:

1. Assume the number of sales is in cell AN1, feedback score is in AN2, and years with the company is in AN3.

2. Click on a cell where you want the bonus eligibility decision to appear.

3. Type **=IF(AND(AN1 > 50, AN2 > 4.5), "Eligible", IF(AN3 > 5, "Eligible", "Not Eligible")).**

4. Press Enter.

5. The cell will display "Eligible" if the conditions for the bonus are met and "Not Eligible" otherwise.

Variations:

- **Using OR Alone:** To check if a sales rep is either a top seller OR has high feedback: **=IF(OR(AN1 > 100, AN2 > 4.8), "Top Performer", "Regular").**

- **Combining AND with OR:** For more complex conditions, you can nest AND and OR functions. For example, to identify if a sales rep is a veteran with high sales OR a newbie with exceptional feedback: **=IF(OR(AND(AN3 > 10, AN1 > 80), AND(AN3 < 1, AN2 > 4.9)), "Special Mention", "Regular").**

NOT

Description:

The NOT function reverses a logical value. If a condition is TRUE, NOT will return FALSE, and vice versa.

Real-World Example:

In a school's grading system, students who score below 40 are considered to have failed. Using the NOT function, you can easily identify students who haven't failed.

Step-by-step Implementation:

1. Assume a student's score is in cell AO1.

2. Click on a cell where you want the pass/fail indication to appear.

3. Type =IF(NOT(AO1 < 40), "Pass", "Fail").

4. Press Enter.

5. The cell will display "Pass" if the student scored 40 or above and "Fail" otherwise.

Variations:

- **Combining with Other Functions:** The NOT function can be combined with other logical functions to create more complex conditions. For instance, with AND: =IF(AND(AO1 >= 40, NOT(AO1 > 90)), "Average", "Outstanding or Fail") - This checks if a student's score is average, i.e., between 40 and 90.

IFERROR

Description:
The IFERROR function allows you to handle errors in formulas by returning a specified value or formula when the primary formula results in an error.

Real-World Example:
You have a list of prices and quantities in a spreadsheet, and you're calculating the cost per item by dividing the price by the quantity. However, in some cases, the quantity might be zero, which would result in a **#DIV/0!** error. Using IFERROR, you can handle this gracefully, returning "N/A" or another value instead of the error.

Step-by-step Implementation:
1. Assume the price is in cell AP1 and the quantity is in AP2.
2. Click on a cell where you want the cost per item to appear.
3. Type **=IFERROR(AP1 / AP2, "N/A")**.
4. Press Enter.
5. If AP2 is not zero, the cell will display the result of the division. If AP2 is zero, it will display "N/A".

Variations:
- **Different Default Values:** Instead of "N/A", you could return 0, "Not Applicable", or any other value or formula that makes sense in the context.

- **Combining with Other Functions:** IFERROR can be used with virtually any Excel function to handle errors. For instance, with VLOOKUP to return "Not Found" if a lookup value isn't in a list: **=IFERROR(VLOOKUP(AP3, A1:B10, 2, FALSE), "Not Found")**.

SWITCH

Description:

The SWITCH function evaluates an expression and returns a result corresponding to the first matching value from a list of values. It provides an efficient alternative to nested IF functions when dealing with multiple conditions.

Real-World Example:

You're categorizing products based on their IDs. Each ID corresponds to a specific category. Using the SWITCH function, you can quickly determine the category for each product ID.

Step-by-step Implementation:

1. Assume a product ID is in cell AQ1.

2. Click on a cell where you want the product category to appear.

3. Type the following formula:

   =SWITCH(AQ1,

      101, "Electronics",

      102, "Apparel",

      103, "Groceries",

      104, "Furniture",

      "Unknown Category")

4. Press Enter.

5. The cell will display the category corresponding to the product ID in AQ1. If the ID doesn't match any of the listed values, it will display "Unknown Category".

Variations:

- **Nested SWITCH:** For more complex conditions, you can nest SWITCH functions, though in most cases, a single

SWITCH should suffice for clarity and efficiency.

- **Combining with Other Functions:** You can use SWITCH in conjunction with other functions. For example, to categorize products based on price ranges, you could use SWITCH with nested IFs or the LOOKUP function.

IFS

Description:
The IFS function allows you to evaluate multiple conditions and return a value corresponding to the first true condition. It's an alternative to nested IF functions and provides a more streamlined approach when dealing with multiple conditions.

Real-World Example:
You're grading students based on their scores. Students with a score of 90 or above get an 'A', those with 80 or above (but below 90) get a 'B', and so on. Using the IFS function, you can easily determine the grade for each student based on their score.

Step-by-step Implementation:
1. Assume a student's score is in cell AR1.
2. Click on a cell where you want the grade to appear.
3. Type the following formula:

```
=IFS(
    AR1 >= 90, "A",
    AR1 >= 80, "B",
    AR1 >= 70, "C",
    AR1 >= 60, "D",
    AR1 < 60, "F"
)
```

4. Press Enter.
5. The cell will display the grade corresponding to the student's score in AR1.

Variations:
- **Using with Other Functions:** The IFS function can be

combined with other Excel functions for more complex evaluations. For instance, combining IFS with ROUND to determine grading tiers based on rounded scores.

- **Handling No Match:** If none of the conditions in the IFS function are met, the function will return a #N/A error. To handle this gracefully, you can wrap the IFS function with an IFERROR function.

COUNTIF

Description:
The COUNTIF function counts the number of cells within a range that meet a single condition. It's a useful tool for quickly tallying how many times a specific value or range of values appears in a dataset.

Real-World Example:
You're analyzing a survey where participants rated a product on a scale from 1 to 5. You want to know how many participants gave a rating of 5.

Step-by-step Implementation:
1. Assume the range of ratings from the survey is in cells A1:A100.

2. Click on a cell where you want the count of ratings equal to 5 to appear.

3. Type **=COUNTIF(A1:A100, 5)**.

4. Press Enter.

5. The cell will display the count of cells in the range A1:A100 that have a value of 5.

Variations:
- **Using Comparison Operators:** You can also use comparison operators in the criteria. For instance, to count ratings greater than 3: **=COUNTIF(A1:A100, ">3")**.

- **Counting Text:** To count the number of times the word "Excellent" appears: **=COUNTIF(A1:A100, "Excellent")**.

- **Combining with Other Functions:** You can use COUNTIF in conjunction with other functions. For

instance, to get the percentage of ratings that are 5:
=COUNTIF(A1:A100, 5)/COUNT(A1:A100).

SUMIF

Description:
The SUMIF function allows you to sum values in a range based on a single condition. It's particularly useful when you want to aggregate data that meets certain criteria.

Real-World Example:
You have a sales report with a list of products and their corresponding sales. You want to calculate the total sales for a specific product, say "Laptop".

Step-by-step Implementation:
1. Assume the range of products is in cells B1:B100 and the corresponding sales values are in cells C1:C100.

2. Click on a cell where you want the total sales for "Laptop" to appear.

3. Type **=SUMIF(B1:B100, "Laptop", C1:C100)**.

4. Press Enter.

5. The cell will display the total sales for the product "Laptop" based on the data in the range B1:C100.

Variations:
- **Using Comparison Operators:** You can also use comparison operators in the criteria. For instance, to sum sales greater than $500: **=SUMIF(C1:C100, ">500")**.

- **Summing with Multiple Criteria:** For situations where you need to sum based on multiple conditions, you can use the SUMIFS function. For instance, to sum sales of "Laptop" in January: **=SUMIFS(C1:C100, B1:B100, "Laptop", A1:A100, "January")** (assuming A1:A100 contains months).

- **Combining with Other Functions:** SUMIF can be paired with other Excel functions for more complex evaluations, such as averaging the sums or counting the number of sums that meet certain thresholds.

AVERAGEIF

Description:

The AVERAGEIF function calculates the average of numbers in a range based on a single condition. It's beneficial for deriving the mean value of a dataset that meets certain criteria.

Real-World Example:

You have a class of students, and you want to compute the average score of students who passed the exam (i.e., scored more than 50).

Step-by-step Implementation:

1. Assume the range of scores is in cells D1:D100.

2. Click on a cell where you want the average score of passing students to appear.

3. Type **=AVERAGEIF(D1:D100, ">50")**.

4. Press Enter.

5. The cell will display the average score of students who scored more than 50.

Variations:

- **Specifying Average Range:** You can also specify a separate range for averaging if the criteria are applied to a different range. For instance, if you have criteria in column E and values to average in column F: **=AVERAGEIF(E1:E100, ">50", F1:F100)**.

- **Averaging Based on Text Criteria:** To calculate the average score of students who received a "Pass" grade (assuming grades are in column E): **=AVERAGEIF(E1:E100, "Pass", D1:D100)**.

- **Averaging with Multiple Criteria:** If you need to compute the average based on multiple conditions, the

AVERAGEIFS function is your go-to. For instance, to determine the average score of students who passed and are in "Section A": **=AVERAGEIFS(D1:D100, E1:E100, "Pass", F1:F100, "Section A")** (assuming F1:F100 contains section information).

MAXIFS

Description:

The MAXIFS function returns the maximum value among cells specified by a given set of conditions or criteria. It allows you to pinpoint the highest value that meets one or more conditions.

Real-World Example:

In a sales report, you want to find the highest sale made by a particular salesperson, say "John Doe".

Step-by-step Implementation:

1. Assume the range of sales values is in cells G1:G100 and the corresponding salespeople are listed in cells H1:H100.

2. Click on a cell where you want the highest sale by "John Doe" to appear.

3. Type =**MAXIFS(G1:G100, H1:H100, "John Doe")**.

4. Press Enter.

5. The cell will display the highest sale made by "John Doe".

Variations:

- **Multiple Criteria:** You can add more conditions to the function. For instance, to find the highest sale by "John Doe" in the month of "January" (assuming I1:I100 contains months): =**MAXIFS(G1:G100, H1:H100, "John Doe", I1:I100, "January")**.

- **Using Comparison Operators:** Instead of exact matches, you can find values that meet certain thresholds. For example, to find the highest sale below $1000: =**MAXIFS(G1:G100, G1:G100, "<1000")**.

- **Minimum Value with Conditions:** If you're interested in the lowest value that meets certain criteria, you can use the MINIFS function in a similar manner.

CHAPTER 5: LOOKUP & REFERENCE FORMULAS

These formulas play a crucial role when you need to search for specific data points within a dataset or want to reference data from one part of a spreadsheet in another. They bring efficiency and automation to tasks that would otherwise be time-consuming.

Let's start with the widely-used **VLOOKUP** function.

VLOOKUP

Description:
The VLOOKUP function searches for a value in the first column of a table range and returns a value in the same row from a specified column. It's one of the most popular functions in Excel for data retrieval.

Real-World Example:
You have a product list with product IDs and their corresponding prices. You want to find the price of a product with a specific ID.

Step-by-step Implementation:
1. Assume the product IDs are in cells A1:A100 and their corresponding prices are in B1:B100.

2. If you want to find the price of the product with ID "P1234", which is in cell J1, click on a cell where you want the price to appear.

3. Type **=VLOOKUP(J1, A1:B100, 2, FALSE)**.

4. Press Enter.

5. The cell will display the price of the product with ID "P1234".

Variations:
- **Approximate Match:** If you set the last argument to TRUE (or omit it), VLOOKUP will look for an approximate match. This is useful when dealing with ranges or categories.

- **Error Handling:** If VLOOKUP doesn't find the lookup value, it will return an error. You can handle this gracefully using IFERROR: **=IFERROR(VLOOKUP(J1, A1:B100, 2, FALSE), "Not Found")**.

HLOOKUP

Description:

The HLOOKUP function searches for a value in the first row of a table range and returns a value in the same column from a specified row. It works similarly to VLOOKUP but searches horizontally instead of vertically.

Real-World Example:

You have a dataset where months are listed in the first row, and sales figures are listed in subsequent rows for different products. You want to retrieve the sales figure for "Widget A" in the month of "March."

Step-by-step Implementation:

1. Assume the months are listed in cells A1:M1, with sales figures for "Widget A" in cells A2:M2, "Widget B" in A3:M3, and so on.
2. If you want to find the sales of "Widget A" for March, click on a cell where you want the sales figure to appear.
3. Type **=HLOOKUP("March", A1:M3, 2, FALSE)**.
4. Press Enter.
5. The cell will display the sales figure for "Widget A" in March.

Variations:

- **Approximate Match:** Similar to VLOOKUP, if you set the last argument to TRUE (or omit it), HLOOKUP will look for an approximate match.

- **Error Handling:** If HLOOKUP doesn't find the lookup value, it will return an error. This can be managed using IFERROR: **=IFERROR(HLOOKUP("March", A1:M3, 2, FALSE), "Not Found")**.

XLOOKUP

Description:
Introduced in Excel 365 and Excel 2019, XLOOKUP is a versatile and more powerful successor to the VLOOKUP and HLOOKUP functions. It searches for a value in a specified lookup range and returns the corresponding value from another range. Unlike its predecessors, XLOOKUP works both vertically and horizontally, doesn't require the lookup value to be in the first column or row, and has more functionalities.

Real-World Example:
You have a list of products and their corresponding codes and prices. You want to find the price of a product based on its code.

Step-by-step Implementation:
1. Assume the product codes are in cells A1:A100 and their corresponding prices are in cells B1:B100.

2. If you want to find the price of the product with code "C123", which is in cell J1, click on a cell where you want the price to appear.

3. Type **=XLOOKUP(J1, A1:A100, B1:B100)**.

4. Press Enter.

5. The cell will display the price corresponding to the product code "C123".

Variations:
- **Default Value for No Match:** You can specify a value to return if the lookup value is not found: **=XLOOKUP(J1, A1:A100, B1:B100, "Not Found")**.

- **Two-way Lookup:** XLOOKUP can replace both VLOOKUP and HLOOKUP, making it easier to perform two-way lookups.

- **Search Last to First:** You can make XLOOKUP search from the end of the list to the beginning using the optional search_mode argument.

- **Wildcard Characters:** XLOOKUP supports wildcards like * and ? for partial matches.

INDEX

Description:
The INDEX function returns the value of a cell in a specific row and column of a range. It's particularly powerful when combined with other functions like MATCH.

Real-World Example:
You have a matrix of sales data where each row represents a product and each column represents a month. You want to retrieve the sales of a specific product for a particular month.

Step-by-step Implementation:
1. Assume the matrix of sales data is in cells A1:M10, with products listed in rows and months in columns.

2. If you want to find the sales for "Product 3" in "March" (which is the third column), you can use the INDEX function to specify the row and column.

3. Type **=INDEX(A1:M10, 3, 3)** in the desired cell.

4. Press Enter.

5. The cell will display the sales figure for "Product 3" in "March".

Variations:
- **Using with MATCH:** Often, you might not know the exact row or column number. In such cases, you can use MATCH to determine it. For instance, if "Product 3" is in cell N1 and "March" is in cell N2, the formula becomes: **=INDEX(A1:M10, MATCH(N1, A1:A10, 0), MATCH(N2, A1:M1, 0))**.

- **Returning an Entire Row or Column:** If you only specify a row number, INDEX will return the entire row. Similarly, specifying only a column will return the entire column. For instance, **=INDEX(A1:M10, 3,)** will return the entire third row.

- **Using Array Form:** INDEX has an array form that allows you to return multiple values at once, useful for array formulas or dynamic ranges.

MATCH

Description:
The MATCH function searches for a specified item in a range and returns the relative position of that item within the range. It's often used in combination with the INDEX function to perform two-dimensional lookups.

Real-World Example:
You have a list of employees, and you want to determine the position of a specific employee, "Jane Doe," in that list.

Step-by-step Implementation:
1. Assume the list of employees is in cells A1:A100.

2. If you want to determine the position of "Jane Doe" in the list, click on a cell where you want the position to appear.

3. Type =**MATCH("Jane Doe", A1:A100, 0)**.

4. Press Enter.

5. The cell will display the relative position of "Jane Doe" in the list.

Variations:
- **Match Type Options:** The third argument in MATCH determines the type of match:
  - **0**: Exact match.
  - **1**: Less than or equal to (list must be sorted in ascending order).
  - **-1**: Greater than or equal to (list must be sorted in descending order).

- **Horizontal Search:** While the example uses a vertical list, MATCH can also search horizontally in a row.

- **Combined with INDEX:** As mentioned, MATCH is often

paired with INDEX to fetch a specific value from a table. For example, to find the salary of "Jane Doe" where salaries are in column B: **=INDEX(B1:B100, MATCH("Jane Doe", A1:A100, 0))**.

OFFSET

Description:

The OFFSET function returns a reference to a range that is a specific number of rows and columns away from a starting cell or range. It allows dynamic referencing of data, making it especially useful in creating dynamic named ranges, charts, or drop-down lists.

Real-World Example:

You have a dataset where new data is added every month, and you want a cell to always display the most recent month's data.

Step-by-step Implementation:

1. Assume your data starts in cell A1 and extends downwards.

2. To display the most recent month's data, which is the last entry in column A, you can use OFFSET combined with the COUNTA function to count non-empty cells.

3. In a desired cell, type: **=OFFSET(A1, COUNTA(A:A)-1, 0)**.

4. Press Enter.

5. The cell will now display the value of the last non-empty cell in column A.

Variations:

- **Specifying Rows and Columns:** The basic syntax of OFFSET is **OFFSET(reference, rows, cols, [height], [width])**. You can adjust the "rows" and "cols" arguments to move up/down and left/right from the reference cell.

- **Dynamic Ranges:** OFFSET can be used to create dynamic named ranges that automatically adjust as data is added or removed. For example, if you want a named range that includes all data in column A: **=OFFSET($A**

$1,0,0,COUNTA($A:$A),1).

- **Combined with Other Functions:** OFFSET can be paired with functions like SUM, AVERAGE, and MAX to perform calculations on dynamic ranges.

CHOOSE

Description:
The CHOOSE function allows you to select one of up to 254 values based on an index number. It's like a simpler, more direct form of the VLOOKUP function for a predefined list.

Real-World Example:
You're creating a simple dashboard where a user can select a month by number (1 for January, 2 for February, etc.), and you want to display the month's name.

Step-by-step Implementation:
1. Assume the user inputs the month number in cell B1.

2. In the cell where you want the month name to appear, type the following:

=CHOOSE(B1, "January", "February", "March", "April", "May", "June", "July", "August", "September", "October", "November", "December")

3. Press Enter.

4. Now, if the user enters "3" in cell B1, the chosen cell will display "March".

Variations:

- **Using with Other Functions:** CHOOSE can be combined with functions like INDEX and MATCH for more complex selections.

- **Returning Ranges:** CHOOSE can also return references to ranges, not just values. For example, if you have data for each month in separate columns, you can use CHOOSE to select the appropriate column based on the month number.

- **Nested CHOOSE Functions:** For more complex scenarios, you can nest multiple CHOOSE functions to create a decision tree-like structure.

GETPIVOTDATA

Description:

The GETPIVOTDATA function extracts specific data from a PivotTable report, allowing you to retrieve summarized data dynamically. It's especially useful for creating custom reports or dashboards based on PivotTable data.

Real-World Example:

You have a PivotTable summarizing sales by product and region. You want to display the sales figure for the product "Laptop" in the "West" region in a separate cell.

Step-by-step Implementation:

1. Assume your PivotTable is placed in cells A1:D20, with products listed in column A and regions in the headers of columns B to D.

2. Click on the cell where you want the sales figure for "Laptop" in the "West" region to appear.

3. Type:

=GETPIVOTDATA("Sales",A1,"Product","Laptop","Region","West")

4. Press Enter.

5. The cell will now display the sales figure for "Laptop" in the "West" region based on the PivotTable.

Variations:

- **Dynamic Retrieval:** You can replace hard-coded values with cell references. For instance, if you have "Laptop" in cell F1 and "West" in cell G1, the formula becomes:

=GETPIVOTDATA("Sales",A1,"Product",F1,"Region",G1)

- **Multiple Criteria:** You can add more criteria pairs to extract data based on multiple conditions.

- **Error Handling:** If GETPIVOTDATA doesn't find the specified data, it will return an error. This can be managed using IFERROR:

=IFERROR(GETPIVOTDATA("Sales",A1,"Product",F1,"Region",G1), "Data Not Found")

INDIRECT

Description:
The INDIRECT function returns a reference specified by a text string. This allows for dynamic referencing of cells, ranges, and even other sheets or workbooks. It's particularly useful when you want to change a formula's reference without altering the formula itself.

Real-World Example:
You're building a dashboard where the user can select a month from a dropdown list, and you want to pull data from a sheet corresponding to the selected month.

Step-by-step Implementation:
1. Assume you have separate sheets named "January", "February", "March", etc., and each sheet has a total sales figure in cell B5.

2. In your dashboard sheet, let's say the user selects "March" from a dropdown list in cell A1.

3. In the cell where you want the sales figure for March to appear, type:

scssCopy code

```
=INDIRECT(A1 & "!B5")
```

4. Press Enter.

5. The cell will now pull the sales figure from cell B5 of the "March" sheet.

Variations:
- **Dynamic Ranges:** INDIRECT can be combined with other functions like COUNTA to create dynamic ranges. For example, to sum all values in column A of the "March" sheet, you could use:

lessCopy code

```
=SUM(INDIRECT(A1 & "!A1:A" & COUNTA(INDIRECT(A1 & "!
A:A"))))
```

- **Reference Other Workbooks:** INDIRECT can also reference other workbooks. If you have a workbook named "SalesData.xlsx" and you want to pull data from cell B5 of the "Summary" sheet, you'd use:

cssCopy code

```
=INDIRECT("[SalesData.xlsx]Summary!B5")
```

- **R1C1 Reference Style:** By default, INDIRECT uses the A1 reference style. But you can also use the R1C1 style by setting the optional second argument to TRUE.

CHAPTER 6: TEXT FORMULAS

Text functions in Excel are incredibly handy for managing and manipulating string data. These functions allow you to extract, combine, transform, or analyze text entries in various ways.

Starting with the **CONCATENATE** and **TEXTJOIN** functions:

CONCATENATE / TEXTJOIN

Description:
The CONCATENATE function combines multiple text strings into one. While CONCATENATE is widely used, Excel introduced the TEXTJOIN function, which offers more flexibility by allowing you to specify a delimiter and handle empty cells.

Real-World Example:
You have first names in column A, last names in column B, and you want to create full names in column C.

Step-by-step Implementation:
1. Assuming you're working with row 1, in cell C1, type for CONCATENATE:

=CONCATENATE(A1, " ", B1)

Or for TEXTJOIN:

=TEXTJOIN(" ", TRUE, A1, B1)

2. Press Enter.

3. Drag down to apply for all rows. Column C will now display full names.

Variations:
- **Using Delimiters:** With TEXTJOIN, you can easily specify different delimiters like commas, dashes, etc.

- **Ignoring Empty Cells:** TEXTJOIN's second argument, when set to TRUE, will skip any empty cells in the range.

LEFT, RIGHT, & MID

Description:
These functions allow you to extract specific characters from a text string.

- **LEFT**: Extracts a specified number of characters from the beginning of a string.

- **RIGHT**: Extracts a specified number of characters from the end of a string.

- **MID**: Extracts a specified number of characters from a string starting at a position you define.

Real-World Example:
You have a list of product codes where the first two characters indicate the product category, the next three characters indicate the manufacturer, and the last three characters are the product number. You want to extract these parts separately.

Step-by-step Implementation:
1. Assume the product code "AB123456" is in cell A1.

2. To extract the product category, in B1 type: **=LEFT(A1, 2)**. This will return "AB".

3. To extract the manufacturer code, in C1 type: **=MID(A1, 3, 3)**. This will return "123".

4. To extract the product number, in D1 type: **=RIGHT(A1, 3)**. This will return "456".

Variations:
- **Dynamic Length Extraction:** If the length of the part you want to extract isn't fixed, you can combine these functions with others like FIND or SEARCH. For example, if you want to extract everything before a

comma in a string, you might use **=LEFT(A1, FIND(",", A1)-1)**.

- **Nested Extractions:** You can nest MID (or any of these functions) within each other to extract more complex patterns.

LEN

Description:
The LEN function returns the number of characters in a text string, including spaces, numbers, and special characters.

Real-World Example:
You're reviewing a list of product descriptions and want to ensure that none exceed 50 characters to fit within a specific display on a website.

Step-by-step Implementation:
1. Assume the product description is in cell A1.

2. To determine the length of the description, click on a cell where you want the character count to appear.

3. Type **=LEN(A1)**.

4. Press Enter.

5. The cell will display the number of characters in the product description from A1.

Variations:
- **Combining with IF for Checks:** You can use LEN in combination with logical functions. For instance, to check if the description in A1 exceeds 50 characters: **=IF(LEN(A1) > 50, "Too long", "Acceptable")**.

- **Ignoring Spaces:** If you want to count characters but ignore spaces, you can subtract the count of spaces from the total length: **=LEN(A1) - LEN(SUBSTITUTE(A1, " ", ""))**.

FIND & SEARCH

Description:
Both FIND and SEARCH functions return the starting position of a specific string within another string. The primary difference is that FIND is case-sensitive and does not allow wildcard characters, whereas SEARCH is not case-sensitive and permits wildcards.

Real-World Example:
You're analyzing customer feedback and want to identify comments that mention "shipping".

Step-by-step Implementation:
1. Assume the customer comment is in cell A1.

2. To determine if "shipping" is mentioned and find its position, click on a cell where you want the result to appear.

3. For a case-sensitive search, type: **=FIND("shipping", A1)**. For a case-insensitive search, type: **=SEARCH("shipping", A1)**.

4. Press Enter.

5. If "shipping" is found, the cell will display the starting position of the word in the comment. If not found, the formula will return an error.

Variations:
- **Handling Errors:** To handle the error when the text is not found, you can wrap the formula in an IFERROR function: **=IFERROR(FIND("shipping", A1), "Not found")**.

- **Using Wildcards with SEARCH:** If you want to find any word starting with "ship", you can use:

=SEARCH("ship*", A1).

REPLACE & SUBSTITUTE

Description:

These functions allow you to replace parts of a text string with another string.

- **REPLACE**: Replaces characters within text at a specific position and for a specific length.

- **SUBSTITUTE**: Replaces a specific string with another throughout the text.

Real-World Example:

You have a list of phone numbers formatted as "123-456-7890" and you want to replace the dashes with spaces.

Step-by-step Implementation:

1. Assume the phone number "123-456-7890" is in cell A1.

2. To replace the dashes with spaces, click on a cell where you want the reformatted number to appear.

3. Type **=SUBSTITUTE(A1, "-", " ")**.

4. Press Enter.

5. The cell will now display "123 456 7890".

Variations:

- **Replacing Specific Occurrences with SUBSTITUTE**: If you only want to replace the first dash, you can use: **=SUBSTITUTE(A1, "-", " ", 1)**.

- **Using REPLACE for Specific Positions**: If you know the exact position and length of the text you want to replace, use the REPLACE function. For example, to replace the first three characters: **=REPLACE(A1, 1, 3, "ABC")**.

UPPER, LOWER, & PROPER

Description:
These functions allow you to change the case of text in Excel.

- **UPPER**: Converts all characters in a text string to uppercase.

- **LOWER**: Converts all characters in a text string to lowercase.

- **PROPER**: Converts the first letter of each word in a text string to uppercase and the rest to lowercase.

Real-World Example:
You have a list of names entered in various text cases and you want to standardize them for a formal document.

Step-by-step Implementation:
1. Assume the name "jOhN dOe" is in cell A1.

2. To convert the name to proper case, click on a cell where you want the standardized name to appear.

3. Type =**PROPER(A1)**.

4. Press Enter.

5. The cell will now display "John Doe".

Variations:
- **Using UPPER for All Caps**: If you want to ensure all characters are uppercase, use: =**UPPER(A1)**. This would return "JOHN DOE".

- **Using LOWER for All Lowercase**: If you want all characters in lowercase, use: =**LOWER(A1)**. This would return "john doe".

TRIM & CLEAN

Description:
These functions help in cleaning up text data in Excel.

- **TRIM**: Removes any leading, trailing, and excessive inline spaces from a text string.

- **CLEAN**: Removes non-printable characters from a text string, which can sometimes appear when importing data from other sources.

Real-World Example:
You've imported a list of email addresses into Excel, but some have extra spaces before, after, or between characters. Additionally, some entries contain non-printable characters causing display issues.

Step-by-step Implementation:
1. Assume the email address " johndoe @example .com " with extra spaces and possible non-printable characters is in cell A1.

2. To clean and trim the email address, click on a cell where you want the cleaned email to appear.

3. Type =**TRIM(CLEAN(A1))**.

4. Press Enter.

5. The cell will now display "johndoe@example.com", cleaned of any non-printable characters and unnecessary spaces.

Variations:
- **Using TRIM Alone**: If you only want to remove spaces without worrying about non-printable characters, simply use: =**TRIM(A1)**.

- **Using CLEAN Alone**: If non-printable characters are the only concern, use: **=CLEAN(A1)**.

TEXT

Description:

The TEXT function allows you to convert a number to text in a specific number format. It's especially useful when you want to display numbers in a certain way within a text string or when combining numbers with text.

Real-World Example:

You're preparing a monthly report and want to create a header like "Sales Report for March 2023".

Step-by-step Implementation:

1. Assume the month number (3 for March) is in cell A1 and the year 2023 is in cell B1.

2. To create the header, click on a cell where you want the header to appear.

3. Type =**"Sales Report for " & TEXT(DATE(B1, A1, 1), "MMMM YYYY")**.

4. Press Enter.

5. The cell will display "Sales Report for March 2023".

Variations:

- **Different Formats**: The TEXT function can handle various formats. For example:
  - Currency: **TEXT(12345.678, "$#,##0.00")** will return "$12,345.68".
  - Percentage: **TEXT(0.25, "0%")** will return "25%".
  - Date: **TEXT(DATE(2023, 3, 15), "dddd, mmmm dd, yyyy")** will return "Wednesday, March 15, 2023".

- **Dynamic Headers**: By linking the TEXT function to cells with variable data, you can create dynamic headers or labels that update automatically based on input.

CHAPTER 7: INFORMATION FORMULAS

Information functions in Excel are used to get information about the content, formatting, location, or type of data in a cell. These functions can help in error-checking, data validation, and more complex calculations.

Starting with the **ISNUMBER** function:

ISNUMBER

Description:
The ISNUMBER function checks if a value is a number and returns TRUE if it is, and FALSE if it isn't.

Real-World Example:
You have a column of data entries, and you want to verify if each entry is a valid number.

Step-by-step Implementation:
1. Assume the data entry is in cell A1.
2. To check if it's a number, click on a cell where you want the result to appear.
3. Type **=ISNUMBER(A1)**.
4. Press Enter.
5. The cell will display TRUE if the content in A1 is a number, and FALSE otherwise.

Variations:
- **Combining with Conditional Formatting**: You can use ISNUMBER in combination with conditional formatting to highlight cells that don't contain valid numbers.

- **Using with Other Functions**: It can be combined with functions like IF to perform specific actions based on whether a cell contains a number.

ISTEXT

Description:

The ISTEXT function checks if a value is text and returns TRUE if it is, and FALSE if it isn't.

Real-World Example:

You're reviewing a dataset of customer names and you want to ensure that all entries in a specific column are text values.

Step-by-step Implementation:

1. Assume the customer name is in cell A1.

2. To verify if it's a text value, click on a cell where you want the result to appear.

3. Type =**ISTEXT(A1)**.

4. Press Enter.

5. The cell will display TRUE if the content in A1 is a text value, and FALSE otherwise.

Variations:

- **Spotting Numbers in Text Columns**: Using ISTEXT can help identify cells that mistakenly contain numbers in columns meant for text data.

- **Conditional Formatting**: Like ISNUMBER, you can also use ISTEXT in combination with conditional formatting to highlight cells that aren't text.

ERROR.TYPE

Description:
The ERROR.TYPE function returns a number corresponding to a specific error type in Excel. This can be helpful for diagnosing and handling different types of errors in your spreadsheets.

Real-World Example:
You have a complex financial model, and occasionally, some cells display errors. You want to categorize these errors for easier troubleshooting.

Step-by-step Implementation:
1. Assume the cell you want to check is A1.

2. To determine the error type, click on a cell where you want the error category to appear.

3. Type =**ERROR.TYPE(A1)**.

4. Press Enter.

5. The cell will display a number corresponding to the error in A1:
    - 1 for **#NULL!**
    - 2 for **#DIV/0!**
    - 3 for **#VALUE!**
    - 4 for **#REF!**
    - 5 for **#NAME?**
    - 6 for **#NUM!**
    - 7 for **#N/A**
    - Returns **#N/A** for any other value.

Variations:
- **Custom Error Messages**: You can use a nested IF or CHOOSE function to provide custom messages

or actions based on the error type. For example: **=CHOOSE(ERROR.TYPE(A1), "Null error", "Division by zero", "Value error", ...)**.

CHAPTER 8: FINANCIAL FORMULAS

Description

PV (PRESENT VALUE)

Description:

The PV function in Excel is used to determine the present value of a loan or an investment based on a constant interest rate and a series of future payments. Essentially, it tells you what a future sum of money is worth in today's terms.

Real-World Example:

Imagine you're considering an investment that promises to pay you $5,000 every year for the next 5 years. If your desired annual interest rate (or discount rate) is 10%, you can use the PV function to find out the present value of this investment.

Step-by-step Implementation:

1. Open a new cell in Excel.

2. Enter the formula: **=PV(10%, 5, -5000)**.

3. Press Enter.

4. The cell will display the present value of the investment, considering the series of future payments and the discount rate.

Note: The payment value is entered as a negative because it represents an outgoing payment from your perspective.

Variations:

- **Including Future Value**: If the investment also has a lump sum payment at the end, this can be added as a future value. For example, if you'll also receive $10,000 at the end of the 5 years, the formula becomes: **=PV(10%, 5, -5000, -10000)**.

- **Monthly Payments**: If payments are made monthly instead of annually, you'd adjust the rate and number of periods accordingly. For an investment with monthly payments of $500 for 5 years: **=PV(10%/12, 5*12, -500)**.

FV (FUTURE VALUE)

Description:

The FV function in Excel is used to determine the future value of an investment based on periodic, constant payments and a constant interest rate. It essentially tells you the worth of a series of present-day payments at a specified date in the future.

Real-World Example:

Imagine you're saving $1,000 every year for the next 5 years in an account that offers a 5% annual interest rate. You can use the FV function to find out the value of your savings at the end of the 5 years.

Step-by-step Implementation:

1. Open a new cell in Excel.

2. Enter the formula: **=FV(5%, 5, -1000)**.

3. Press Enter.

4. The cell will display the future value of your savings, considering the series of deposits and the interest rate.

Note: The payment value is entered as a negative because it represents an outgoing payment from your perspective.

Variations:

- **Starting with an Initial Amount**: If you already have an initial amount saved (let's say $5,000), this can be added as a present value. The formula becomes: **=FV(5%, 5, -1000, -5000)**.

- **Monthly Deposits**: If you're depositing monthly instead of annually, adjust the rate and number of periods. For monthly deposits of $100 for 5 years: **=FV(5%/12, 5*12, -100)**.

NPV (NET PRESENT VALUE)

Description:
The NPV function calculates the net present value of an investment based on a series of anticipated future cash inflows and a discount rate. It helps in determining the potential profitability of an investment.

Real-World Example:
Imagine you're considering a project that requires an initial investment of $10,000 today and is expected to generate cash inflows of $4,000 at the end of the first year, $5,000 at the end of the second year, and $6,000 at the end of the third year. If your desired annual discount rate is 8%, you can use the NPV function to assess the project's worth.

Step-by-step Implementation:
1. Place the future cash inflows in cells A1, A2, and A3 (i.e., 4000, 5000, 6000).
2. In a new cell, type the formula: **=NPV(8%, A1:A3) - 10000**.
3. Press Enter.
4. The cell will display the net present value of the project. A positive NPV indicates a potentially profitable investment, while a negative NPV suggests it might not be worth pursuing.

Variations:
- **Variable Discount Rates**: If you anticipate that the discount rate might change annually, you could use a combination of the NPV function with other functions

to account for this.

- **Incorporating Costs**: If there are anticipated costs in the future, they should be entered as negative values in the cash inflow series.

IRR (INTERNAL RATE OF RETURN)

Description:
The IRR function calculates the internal rate of return for a series of cash flows, which represents the expected growth of an investment. It is especially useful in capital budgeting to compare the profitability of different investments.

Real-World Example:
You're evaluating a project that requires an initial investment of $10,000 and is projected to generate returns of $4,000 at the end of the first year, $5,000 at the end of the second year, and $6,000 at the end of the third year. By calculating the IRR, you can determine the project's annualized rate of return.

Step-by-step Implementation:
1. Place the cash flows in cells starting from A1: -10000 (initial investment), 4000, 5000, 6000.

2. In a new cell, type the formula: **=IRR(A1:A4)**.

3. Press Enter.

4. The cell will display the internal rate of return for the project as a decimal. Multiply by 100 to get the percentage.

Variations:
- **Guess Value**: The IRR function can sometimes have multiple solutions, especially with non-conventional cash flows. You can provide an initial guess for the IRR to help Excel find the most appropriate solution. For instance: **=IRR(A1:A4, 0.1)** where 0.1 (or 10%) is the guess.

- **Monthly Cash Flows**: If you're working with monthly cash flows, you'll arrange them in sequential cells and apply the IRR function similarly.

PMT (PAYMENT)

Description:

The PMT function calculates the payment for a loan based on constant payments and a constant interest rate. It's commonly used for calculating mortgage or car loan payments.

Real-World Example:

You're planning to take out a car loan for $20,000. The loan term is 5 years (or 60 months), and the annual interest rate is 5%. You want to know what your monthly payment will be.

Step-by-step Implementation:

1. Open a new cell in Excel.

2. Enter the formula: **=PMT(5%/12, 60, 20000)**.

3. Press Enter.

4. The cell will display the monthly payment you'll need to make. The result will be a negative number, representing an outgoing payment.

Variations:

- **Total Interest Over Loan Term**: To calculate the total interest you'll pay over the term of the loan, you can multiply the PMT result by the total number of payments and then add the loan amount: **= (PMT(5%/12, 60, 20000) * 60) + 20000**.

- **Annual Payments**: If you're making yearly instead of monthly payments, adjust the rate and number of periods. For instance, for annual payments on the same loan: **=PMT(5%, 5, 20000)**.

RATE (INTEREST RATE OF ANNUITY)

Description:

The RATE function in Excel determines the interest rate per period of an annuity. It's useful for finding out the interest rate required to save a specific amount of money or repay a loan over a specified time frame.

Real-World Example:

Suppose you're saving $200 every month in a savings account, aiming to accumulate $15,000 after 5 years (or 60 months). You want to determine the monthly interest rate you'll need to achieve this goal.

Step-by-step Implementation:
1. Open a new cell in Excel.

2. Enter the formula: **=RATE(60, -200, 0, 15000)**.

3. Press Enter.

4. The cell will display the monthly interest rate (as a decimal) needed to reach your savings goal. To get the rate as a percentage, multiply the result by 100.

Variations:
- **Loan Repayment**: The RATE function can also determine the interest rate needed to repay a specific loan amount over a set number of periods. If you borrowed $10,000 and plan to repay it in $250 monthly payments over 5 years, the formula becomes: **=RATE(60, -250, 10000)**.

- **Annual Savings**: If you're saving annually instead of

monthly, adjust the number of periods and payment amount accordingly.

NPER (NUMBER OF PERIODS)

Description:

The NPER function calculates the number of periods for an investment or loan based on constant periodic payments, a constant interest rate, and a target future value.

Real-World Example:

You've taken a loan of $10,000 with a monthly interest rate of 5% and are making monthly payments of $200. You want to determine how long it will take to repay the loan fully.

Step-by-step Implementation:

1. Open a new cell in Excel.

2. Enter the formula: **=NPER(5%/12, -200, 10000)**.

3. Press Enter.

4. The cell will display the number of months required to repay the loan with the specified monthly payment and interest rate.

Variations:

- **Savings Goal**: The NPER function can also be used to determine how many periods it will take to reach a specific savings goal. For instance, if you're saving $300 monthly with an annual interest rate of 6% and aim to accumulate $20,000, the formula becomes: **=NPER(6%/12, -300, 0, 20000)**.

- **Different Compounding Periods**: If interest compounds quarterly or annually, adjust the rate and payment inputs to match the compounding period.

CHAPTER 9: STATISTICAL FORMULAS

AVERAGE

Description:
The AVERAGE function calculates the arithmetic mean of a set of values. It sums up all the numbers in a range and then divides the sum by the count of numbers.

Real-World Example:
You have scores from five tests: 85, 90, 78, 88, and 92. You want to find out your average score across these tests.

Step-by-step Implementation:
1. Enter the test scores in cells A1 through A5.

2. In a new cell, type the formula: **=AVERAGE(A1:A5)**.

3. Press Enter.

4. The cell will display the average score of the five tests.

Variations:
- **Ignoring Zero**: If you want to calculate the average but ignore zero values, you can use the AVERAGEIF function: **=AVERAGEIF(A1:A5, "<>0")**.

- **Weighted Average**: If each test has a different weight or significance, you can calculate a weighted average by multiplying each test score by its weight, summing those products, and then dividing by the total weight.

MEDIAN

Description:
The MEDIAN function calculates the middle value in a dataset. It's useful for finding the midpoint of a set of numbers, which can be more robust to extreme values than the mean (average).

Real-World Example:
You want to determine the median income in a group of people to understand the income distribution more accurately.

Step-by-step Implementation:
1. Enter the income values in cells A1 through A10.

2. In a new cell, type the formula: **=MEDIAN(A1:A10)**.

3. Press Enter.

4. The cell will display the median income of the ten individuals.

Variations:
- **Handling Even Sets**: If you have an even number of data points, the median is calculated as the average of the two middle values. Excel handles this automatically.

- **Median for Categorical Data**: The MEDIAN function can also be used to find the middle value in a list of non-numeric data, such as names or categories.

MODE

Description:

The MODE function calculates the most frequently occurring value in a dataset. It's helpful for finding the value that appears most often.

Real-World Example:

You have a list of test scores for a class of students, and you want to know the most common test score.

Step-by-step Implementation:

1. Enter the test scores in cells A1 through A20.

2. In a new cell, type the formula: **=MODE(A1:A20)**.

3. Press Enter.

4. The cell will display the test score that appears most frequently.

Variations:

- **Multiple Modes**: If there's more than one mode (i.e., multiple values that occur most frequently), the MODE function returns the lowest mode. You can use additional functions or techniques to find all modes if needed.

STDEV.P (POPULATION STANDARD DEVIATION)

Description:
The STDEV.P function calculates the standard deviation for a population based on a sample of data. It measures how spread out the data points are from the mean. A low standard deviation indicates that the data points are close to the mean, while a high standard deviation suggests they are more dispersed.

Real-World Example:
You want to understand the variability in the daily returns of a stock over the past year to assess its risk. You have daily return data in cells A1 through A365.

Step-by-step Implementation:
1. Enter the daily return data in cells A1 through A365.

2. In a new cell, type the formula: **=STDEV.P(A1:A365)**.

3. Press Enter.

4. The cell will display the population standard deviation of the daily returns.

Variations:
- **Sample Standard Deviation**: If your data represents a sample from a larger population (e.g., a sample of 30 out of 100), you would use the STDEV.S function to calculate the sample standard deviation.

CORREL (CORRELATION COEFFICIENT)

Description:

The CORREL function calculates the correlation coefficient between two sets of data. It measures the strength and direction of the linear relationship between two variables. The result is a value between -1 and 1, where -1 indicates a strong negative correlation, 0 indicates no correlation, and 1 indicates a strong positive correlation.

Real-World Example:

You have data for the number of hours spent studying and the corresponding test scores for a group of students. You want to determine if there's a correlation between study time and test scores.

Step-by-step Implementation:

1. Enter the study time data in cells A1 through A10 and the test scores in cells B1 through B10.

2. In a new cell, type the formula: **=CORREL(A1:A10, B1:B10)**.

3. Press Enter.

4. The cell will display the correlation coefficient between study time and test scores.

Interpretation:

- A positive correlation coefficient (close to 1) suggests that as one variable increases, the other tends to increase as well.

- A negative correlation coefficient (close to -1) suggests that as one variable increases, the other tends to decrease.
- A correlation coefficient close to 0 suggests little to no linear relationship between the variables.

QUARTILE (QUARTILES OF A DATA SET)

Description:

The QUARTILE function helps identify values that divide a dataset into quartiles. Quartiles are values that separate a dataset into four equal parts, each containing 25% of the data. There are three quartiles: Q1 (25th percentile), Q2 (50th percentile, or the median), and Q3 (75th percentile).

Real-World Example:

You have a dataset of sales figures for a retail store, and you want to determine the values that represent the 25th, 50th, and 75th percentiles to understand the distribution of sales.

Step-by-step Implementation:

1. Enter the sales data in cells A1 through A50.

2. In a new cell, type the formula for the 25th percentile (Q1): **=QUARTILE(A1:A50, 1)**.

3. In another cell, type the formula for the 50th percentile (Q2 or the median): **=QUARTILE(A1:A50, 2)**.

4. In yet another cell, type the formula for the 75th percentile (Q3): **=QUARTILE(A1:A50, 3)**.

Press Enter after each formula.

5. The cells will display the values representing the specified quartiles.

Interpretation:

- Q1 (25th percentile) is the value below which 25% of the data falls.

- Q2 (50th percentile or median) is the value below which

50% of the data falls.

- Q3 (75th percentile) is the value below which 75% of the data falls.

CHAPTER 10: ARRAY FORMULAS

Array Formulas

Description:

Array formulas in Excel allow you to perform multiple calculations on one or more items in an array. Unlike regular formulas that work with single values, array formulas can process multiple values simultaneously. They are particularly useful when dealing with large datasets or complex calculations.

Real-World Example:

Imagine you have a dataset with sales figures and corresponding quantities sold. You want to find the total revenue for each product (sales amount multiplied by quantity) and then calculate the overall total revenue.

Step-by-step Implementation for SUMPRODUCT (Array Formula):

1. Enter the sales figures in cells A1 to A10 and the quantities sold in cells B1 to B10.

2. In a new cell, type the formula: **=SUMPRODUCT(A1:A10, B1:B10)**.

3. Press Enter.

4. The cell will display the total revenue, calculated as the sum of (sales amount * quantity) for each row.

Note: You don't need to enter array formulas with Ctrl+Shift+Enter anymore (as in older Excel versions); Excel automatically recognizes array formulas and handles them accordingly.

Benefits:

- Array formulas streamline complex calculations and

reduce the need for additional helper columns.

- They can perform multiple calculations in a single formula, saving time and improving spreadsheet efficiency.

Array Formula Best Practices:

- Use array formulas when necessary for complex calculations or when working with large datasets.

- Be cautious with array formulas as they can slow down workbook performance with extensive use.

- Understand the logic of array formulas before applying them to your data.

TRANSPOSE (TRANSPOSE A RANGE OR ARRAY)

Description:
The TRANSPOSE function is used to switch the rows and columns of a range or array. It can be particularly useful when you need to reorganize data for different types of analysis or presentation.

Real-World Example:
You have a dataset with sales figures organized in rows, and you want to switch it to a columnar format for a different analysis.

Step-by-step Implementation for TRANSPOSE:
1. Select the destination range where you want to transpose the data. Ensure it has the same number of cells as the original range, but with switched rows and columns.

2. In the destination range, type the formula: **=TRANSPOSE(OriginalRange)**, where "OriginalRange" is the range you want to transpose.

3. Instead of pressing Enter, you should press **Ctrl+Shift+Enter** because this is an array formula.

Interpretation:
- The TRANSPOSE function flips the rows and columns of a range or array, effectively changing the orientation of your data.

Note:
- When using TRANSPOSE, ensure that the destination range is of the appropriate size to accommodate the

transposed data.

Benefits:

- TRANSPOSE simplifies the process of switching data between row and column formats.

- It's handy for reformatting data for various purposes, such as charting, data analysis, or reporting.

INDEX (RETRIEVE A VALUE FROM AN ARRAY)

Description:

The INDEX function is used to retrieve a value from a specific location within an array or range. It's commonly used in combination with the MATCH function for advanced lookups.

Real-World Example:

You have a table of products and their corresponding prices. You want to find the price of a specific product by searching for its name.

Step-by-step Implementation for INDEX:

1. Assume your product names are in cells A1 to A10, and their prices are in cells B1 to B10.

2. In a new cell, type the formula: **=INDEX(B1:B10, Match("Product Name", A1:A10, 0))**.

3. Replace "Product Name" with the actual name of the product you're searching for.

4. Press Enter.

5. The cell will display the price of the specified product.

MATCH (FIND THE POSITION OF A VALUE IN A RANGE)

Description:

The MATCH function is used to find the position of a specified value within a range. It's often used to locate the row or column number for INDEX function purposes.

Real-World Example:

You want to find the position of a specific product name within a list of products.

Step-by-step Implementation for MATCH:

1. Assume your product names are in cells A1 to A10, and you want to find the position of "Product Name."

2. In a new cell, type the formula: **=MATCH("Product Name", A1:A10, 0)**.

3. Replace "Product Name" with the actual name of the product you're searching for.

4. Press Enter.

5. The cell will display the position of the specified product within the range.

Benefits:

- INDEX and MATCH together provide advanced lookup capabilities, enabling you to search for and retrieve specific values from large datasets efficiently.

- They are versatile and can handle both horizontal and vertical lookups.

CHAPTER 11: DYNAMIC ARRAYS & SPILL FORMULAS

Dynamic Arrays & Spill Formulas
Description:
Dynamic arrays and spill formulas are a set of powerful features introduced in newer versions of Excel (Excel 365 and Excel 2019) that allow functions to return multiple results and automatically "spill" those results into adjacent cells. This simplifies complex calculations and data analysis tasks.

Dynamic Array Functions Covered:
1. **FILTER**: Filters data based on specified criteria and spills the matching results into adjacent cells.

2. **SORT**: Sorts a range of data and spills the sorted results into adjacent cells.

3. **UNIQUE**: Extracts unique values from a range and spills them into adjacent cells.

Real-World Example:
Imagine you have a large dataset of sales transactions, and you want to filter, sort, and extract unique product names from it.

Step-by-step Implementation for FILTER (Dynamic Array Function):
1. Enter your dataset in a range.

2. In an adjacent cell, type the formula: **=FILTER(DataRange, Criteria)**, where "DataRange" is the range containing your data, and "Criteria" specifies the filtering conditions.

3. Press Enter, and the matching results will automatically spill into adjacent cells.

Step-by-step Implementation for SORT (Dynamic Array Function):

1. Enter your dataset in a range.

2. In an adjacent cell, type the formula: **=SORT(DataRange, [SortColumn], [SortOrder])**, where "DataRange" is the range to be sorted, and you can specify optional sorting parameters.

3. Press Enter, and the sorted results will automatically spill into adjacent cells.

Step-by-step Implementation for UNIQUE (Dynamic Array Function):

1. Enter your dataset in a range.

2. In an adjacent cell, type the formula: **=UNIQUE(DataRange, [ByColumn], [ExactlyOnce])**, where "DataRange" is the range containing your data, and you can specify optional parameters.

3. Press Enter, and the unique values will automatically spill into adjacent cells.

Benefits:

· Dynamic arrays and spill formulas simplify complex data tasks by automatically handling multiple results.

· They reduce the need for complicated array formulas and make spreadsheet modeling more intuitive.

Note:

· These dynamic array functions are available in newer Excel versions, and their behavior may differ in older versions.

CHAPTER 12:
DATABASE FORMULAS

Database Formulas

Description:

Database formulas in Excel are designed to work with structured data organized in tables or databases. These formulas allow you to perform calculations and retrieve information from specific rows that meet certain criteria.

Key Database Functions:

1. **DSUM**: Calculates the sum of values in a database that meet specified criteria.

2. **DAVERAGE**: Calculates the average of values in a database that meet specified criteria.

3. **DCOUNT**: Counts the number of records in a database that meet specified criteria.

Real-World Example:

Imagine you have a database of employee information, and you want to calculate the total salary of employees in the Sales department, their average age, and count the number of employees meeting this criteria.

Step-by-step Implementation for DSUM (Database Function):

1. Ensure your data is organized in a table or database format.

2. Create a criteria range that specifies the criteria for selecting records (e.g., department = "Sales").

3. In separate cells, you can use DSUM to calculate the sum of specific columns that meet the criteria.

Step-by-step Implementation for
DAVERAGE (Database Function):

1. Similar to DSUM, ensure your data is organized in a table or database format.

2. Create a criteria range that specifies the criteria for selecting records.

3. Use DAVERAGE to calculate the average of specific columns that meet the criteria.

Step-by-step Implementation for
DCOUNT (Database Function):

1. Again, ensure your data is organized in a table or database format.

2. Create a criteria range specifying the criteria for selecting records.

3. Use DCOUNT to count the number of records that meet the criteria.

Benefits:

- Database formulas are essential for performing calculations and extracting information from structured datasets.

- They are particularly useful in scenarios where you need to analyze and report on specific subsets of data.

Note:

- Ensure that your data is organized as a table or database to make use of these functions effectively.

CHAPTER 13:
ADVANCED FORMULA
TECHNIQUES

Advanced Formula Techniques

Description:

This chapter explores advanced techniques for working with Excel formulas to enhance your productivity and analysis capabilities. Topics covered include:

1. *Formula Auditing*: Techniques for debugging, tracing precedents and dependents, and evaluating formulas step by step.

2. *Using Named Ranges in Formulas:* How to create and utilize named ranges to make formulas more readable and maintainable.

3. *Conditional Formatting with Formulas*: Applying conditional formatting rules based on formula conditions to highlight specific data points.

4. *Array Formulas*: Delving deeper into array formulas, understanding their capabilities, and applying them effectively.

5. *Data Validation with Custom Formulas*: Creating custom validation rules using formulas to control data input.

6. *Dynamic Formulas with OFFSET and INDIRECT:* Learning to build dynamic formulas that adapt to changing data using OFFSET and INDIRECT functions.

Real-World Example:

You have a large dataset with financial transactions, and you want to set up conditional formatting rules to highlight transactions that exceed a certain threshold, all while using named ranges for clarity.

Step-by-step Implementation for Conditional Formatting with Formulas:

1. Select the range of cells containing financial transaction values.

2. Go to the "Home" tab and click "Conditional Formatting."

3. Choose "New Rule" and select "Use a formula to determine which cells to format."

4. Enter the formula that defines your condition (e.g., **=B2>1000** to highlight transactions over $1,000).

5. Specify the formatting options (e.g., font color or cell fill color) for cells meeting the condition.

6. Click "OK" to apply the conditional formatting.

Benefits:

- Advanced formula techniques help streamline data analysis, make formulas more readable, and allow for dynamic data handling.

- They are essential for creating interactive and informative spreadsheets.

Note:

- These advanced techniques require a good understanding of Excel functions and formulas.

CHAPTER 14:
CONCLUSION AND
BEST PRACTICES

Conclusion and Best Practices

Summary:

In this comprehensive guide, we've explored the world of Excel formulas, from the basics to advanced techniques. We've covered everything from simple arithmetic calculations to advanced functions like DSUM and dynamic array formulas. As we conclude, let's recap the key takeaways and best practices for effectively using Excel formulas.

Key Takeaways:

1. **Start with the Basics**: Build a strong foundation by understanding basic arithmetic, operators, and functions like SUM, AVERAGE, and IF.

2. **Master Functions**: Explore and practice with various Excel functions to perform a wide range of calculations and data manipulations.

3. **Structured Data**: Organize your data in tables or databases to maximize the efficiency of database functions.

4. **Named Ranges**: Use named ranges to make your formulas more readable and maintainable.

5. **Array Formulas**: Learn how to create and use array formulas for complex calculations.

6. **Dynamic Formulas**: Utilize functions like OFFSET and INDIRECT to create dynamic formulas that adapt to

changing data.

7. **Conditional Formatting**: Apply conditional formatting with formulas to visually highlight important data points.

8. **Data Validation**: Create custom validation rules using formulas to ensure data accuracy.

9. **Advanced Techniques**: Explore advanced formula techniques, including formula auditing and troubleshooting, to become an Excel power user.

Best Practices:

1. **Plan Your Workbook**: Design your workbook with clarity and structure in mind, using named ranges and consistent formatting.

2. **Document Your Formulas**: Add comments or a formula legend to explain complex formulas for yourself and others.

3. **Audit and Validate**: Regularly audit and validate your formulas to catch errors and inconsistencies.

4. **Efficiency Matters**: Optimize your formulas for efficiency, especially when working with large datasets.

5. **Data Backup**: Keep backups of your data, especially when performing complex operations with formulas.

Troubleshooting Tips:

1. Use Excel's built-in tools like "Trace Precedents" and "Evaluate Formula" to debug issues.

2. Check for typos and syntax errors, especially with functions and references.

3. Verify cell references, relative and absolute, to ensure they point to the correct data.

4. Divide complex formulas into smaller, manageable parts for easier troubleshooting.

Continued Learning:

1. Explore online resources, courses, and forums to deepen your Excel formula skills.

2. Consider advanced Excel certifications to showcase your expertise.

3. Stay updated with Excel's latest features and functions, as Microsoft regularly releases updates.

Excel is a Powerful Tool:

Excel is not just a spreadsheet program; it's a powerful tool for data analysis, reporting, and decision-making. By mastering Excel formulas and best practices, you can unlock its full potential.

Resources for Further Learning:

- Microsoft Excel Help Center

- Microsoft Excel Official Blog

- Online courses and tutorials on platforms like Coursera, edX, and LinkedIn Learning.

Conclusion:

With dedication and practice, you can become an Excel formula expert. Remember that Excel is a tool that can significantly boost your productivity and analytical skills. Keep exploring, learning, and applying what you've discovered in this guide to become proficient in Excel formulas.

Thank you for joining us on this Excel formula journey, and we wish you success in your Excel endeavors!